Yoga of Leadership

The secret to sanity in insane times

By Suzi Pomerantz and Linda Stern Lang

Copyright © 2007 by Suzi Pomerantz
Copyright © 2012 by Suzi Pomerantz and Linda Stern Lang
All rights reserved,
including the right of reproduction
in whole or in part in any form.

Available in paperback and as digital book
in the Kindle format.

Acknowledgments

We are grateful for, and thank Jackie Eiting for her significant contributions to this book. Jacs, you're an amazing leader and coach, and your hours of commitment to the premise behind this book and the contribution of your thinking as an early co-author and thought partner in 2008 really helped make it a reality. Thank you!

Many people contributed to the writing process at various stages, and we are grateful for the help, support, and expertise of Bhavesh Naik, Ken Kesslin and Jackie Eiting for being early readers and providing a reality check for us; and to Leslie Stephen for her editing and organizational prowess. And we heartily thank our dear colleague Kathy Thompson, who brought us together in the first place.

Dedications

This book is dedicated to any leader who has ever held her breath; to any leader who thinks he has to get it right all the time; and to all leaders who are learning that to change the world they must first see themselves.

We also dedicate this book to all the others who recognize that yoga is life and yoga is leadership and it's more than just a metaphor.

Suzi's Dedication: To Bruce, Samantha, and Bryan...the loves of my life.

Linda's Dedication: To my children Madelyn, Max and Katrina, who hold me to high standards: clear, honest communication, speaking from the heart and not "dancing around" what is important.

And to Gerry, who has chosen to share his life with me

Yoga of Leadership:

The secret to sanity in insane times

By Suzi Pomerantz and Linda Stern Lang

The practical application of ancient wisdom for those who lead in extraordinarily challenging modern times.

Tired of the normal prescriptions of do more, be more, do it faster, cheaper, better, smarter? Today's leaders need a break! This book shows leaders a way to be powerful and effective in the midst of it all while retaining (or reclaiming) sanity, serenity, and grounded focus.

Yoga provides tools to survive and thrive in an increasingly complex world. Presence of mind, peace, balance, strength, confidence, space, freedom ~ what leader couldn't use more of these? The principles and lessons of yoga have a direct and profound impact on how leaders create and operate their organizations and themselves, even if those leaders never take up the physical practice of yoga.

THIS BOOK IS FOR YOU IF:

- You are a leader: whether emerging, novice, experienced, or sage.

- You are a leader: whether of a company, a not-for-profit organization, a small business, an initiative, a project, a social movement, politics, a team, a community, a congregation, a family, a group, a life, or yourself.

- You are seeking an easier way to connect to your role as a leader amidst the frenzied pace of business and life today.

- You are overwhelmed, and know there's a better way.

- You want strategies for how to regularly access your inner wisdom and find your voice as a leader without missing a beat in your day-to-day work or life.

- You are anywhere on the yoga spectrum: practicing or not, love yoga or have no idea what yoga is, you keep hearing about it or you've maybe tried one class, you've seen people do yoga, you practice regularly, you teach yoga, you are an enlightened yogi master. Wherever you are on the yoga spectrum, you will find new connections, a new perspective, and a new way of looking at both Yoga and Leadership.

This book could also be subtitled: *The Inner Game of Leading*, since the Yoga of Leadership gives you insight and practices for how to manage your own mind and energy to be most effective as a leader regardless of circumstances in which you find yourself. It's crucial to your success in leadership, whether you are leading a company, your career, a family, a team, or a community. Think of it as a holistic guidebook that takes you to an integrated approach to leadership. Most education for leaders is outside of ourselves. We go to university and graduate school, we read books, we attend trainings and webinars, watch TED talks or attend conferences -- it's all external information coming in from other sources. We have knowledge and wisdom internally that we don't always access or even know how to access in any given situation. That's what this book is about. It's about how to play your inner game of leadership. This book is written for anyone who finds the competing demands of life difficult to balance. It's for people who aspire to leadership and have questions. It's for people who wake up in leadership roles and wonder, "what now?" It's for people who are entrenched in their leadership role and questioning the demands and perks in search of meaning. It's for people who want success without sacrificing inner peace. It's for people who want to know how to operationalize their intuition.

We explore what yoga and leadership have to do with each other. Principles of yoga create harmony, balance, strength, confidence, flexibility, awareness and joy. The tool of awareness is the secret to the way we impact others. Everything comes from it: motivation, leading others, mastering yourself, making a difference, getting results. Yoga of Leadership is access to that awareness of yourself as a leader.

Table of Contents

Welcome to The Yoga of Leadership 1

    What to Expect 6

    What to Know 7

Introduction: We begin 9

    The Secret to Sanity in Insane Times 9

    The Bottom Line 14

Chapter 1 Executive Presence: The Outer Expression of Inner Intention 19

    Innovative Influence and Transformational Relationships 20

    The Total Expression of Self: Executive Presence 21

    ASANA #1: TADASANA (Mountain Pose) 24

    Try It Yourself! 25

    How to Practice Mountain Pose: 28

    Reflections: Self-Observation, Self-awareness 30

    Balanced Awareness: The Ability to Organize Action from Within.. 31

    Timing: The first look at Patience 32

Chapter Two Executive Insight The Art of Balanced Awareness: Inner Intention and Being the "I" of the Storm 33

    ASANA #2: *VRKSASANA* (Tree Pose)..................34
    How to practice Tree Pose: 36
    Repeat using the opposite leg. Breathe. 37
    Creating Stability through Strength 37
    The Mythic Quest for Control..................40
    TRANSITIONAL ASANA: *UTTANASANA* (Intense Stretch/Forward Bend) 41

Chapter Three From Individual Awareness, to Global Perspective 43

    ASANA #4: *Garudasana* - Eagle Pose 43
    How to practice Eagle Pose: 45
    Lead, and Practice, from Your Heart 47
    FEAR, Balanced Awareness, Keen Awareness 47

Chapter Four Leadership as an exercise in Perspective & Preparedness 49

    Asana #5: *Virbhadrasana*, Warrior Pose I 50
    Finding the Edge of Comfort..................53
    Stretching into Your Comfort Zone 53
    Stretched, Comfortable and Being In the Zone 54
    ASANA #6: *Virabhadrasana II*, Heroic Warrior Pose II..................56
    ASANA #7: *Virabhadrasana III*, Warrior III 59
    Stretch Objectives: Moving from the Known to the Unknown..................62
    Finding Center on the Edge 62
    Seeing the Value in Action without Clinging to Expectations..................63

Chapter Five Leadership: Perspective and Self-Preservation 65

    Asana #8: *Setu Banda,* Bridge Pose 66

    How to practice Bridge Pose: 67

    Congruence and Alignment 69

    Power of Inversion 69

    Shifting Leadership Point of View 70

Chapter Six The Dance of Creation and Control, that which a Leader Does Best 72

    Asana #9: *Nataraja* , The Divine Dancer. 74

    How to practice Divine Dancer Pose: 75

    Effortless Engagement 77

Chapter Seven Internal Politics — Residing Within 78

    Asana #10: *Savasana,* (pronounced "shi-vasana") Corpse Pose 78

    How to practice this yoga posture: 79

    Be the Observer 80

    Begin Again: The Ultimate Secrets are Always the Most Obvious, Simple and Magical 83

About The Authors 84

    SUZI POMERANTZ 84

    LINDA LANG 86

Author's Note: 90

Welcome to The Yoga of Leadership

How can you be your best and therefore influence positive change, helping others to be their best? Leadership relationships transform when doing is influenced by being.

Think about creating balance in work and in life ~
simultaneously ~
and about the essential relationship between the way we do things, and who we are.

"Simultaneously" is how things happen, whether beautifully orchestrated or chaotic. When we can stop what we are doing and look carefully into what is happening moment to moment, we become still. In stillness we become aware of what we are doing, so that we can see it clearly for what it is.

Keen awareness arises from paying attention to what you are doing, being fully present, moment to moment. When we can slow down and reside in stillness, it provides space to discover insight to protect ourselves from destructive tendencies, to avoid the confusions and stressors that destroy health and well-being, in an individual or an organization. It gives resiliency and release from the overwhelming aspects of work and life, and it allows us to inspire others.

- we see rich layers of connection between yoga and leadership
- people and societies are stressed beyond measure,
- leadership is elusive or absent

- we appreciate the importance of taking control of our own individual lives, the capacity to lead ourselves into lives of meaning
- When leaders breathe, make new connections, and bring their best self to their role as leader, they impact the bottom line of every entity they lead.

We are passionate about yoga. We are passionate about leadership, and have created the Yoga of Leadership.

Do you wish for greater balance between work and personal life?

Are you seeking simple solutions to dealing with stress and intensity?

Have you developed a keen awareness that adds meaning and value to our life?
And are you ready to sit with this discovery on the virtual yoga mat, to cultivate the inner peace that already resides within you, in the face of the chaos and insanity of modern life?

In essence, can you create a life of meaning, and share that vision to inspire others?

This is how *our* little book becomes *your* little book, with insights about yogic thinking and the qualities of mindful, visionary leadership. It provides an alternative to what the current culture, media and so-called "leadership gurus" are telling us will make us happy, well and satisfied.

DEFINING LEADERSHIP AND YOGA:

First, we must set the stage a bit by attempting to define and harness what leadership is. We all know the word, we have an idea of what it means, yet if we asked you to define it, each of you would come up with a different definition, we're sure of it. So, let's get on the same page before we launch into the Yoga of Leadership, shall we?

Leadership is so broad and deep that there are tens of thousands of books on the subject. Literally. We did a search on Amazon and it showed over 98,000 books on leadership.

If we turn to the dictionary* for the simplest explanation, we find

leadership *n*

1. the office or position of the head of a political party or other body of people

    1. the ability to guide, direct, or influence people

    2. guidance or direction

Encarta® World English Dictionary

If we Google the term "leadership", we are rewarded with nearly 100 million hits. Wikipedia states, "leadership has been described as the "process of social influence in which one person can enlist the aid and support of others in the accomplishment of a common task."

For our purposes, assume leadership is made up of Four A's: Awareness, Authenticity, Alignment and Action.

Awareness is both self-awareness and constantly growing one's awareness of others. It involves being aware of the political landscape around you so that you can successfully navigate and influence others. It involves self-improvement and continual growth to expand and leverage your strengths.

Authenticity is the art of being yourself, honoring your natural personality, and owning your voice and power. Bringing forth your best self in all interactions and being true to yourself and your highest values are key components in strong leadership.

Alignment is the element of aligning your actions and messages with your most profound and meaningful commitments, but it also means mastering the art of bringing other people and resources into alignment with a shared vision. This is how engagement is created and sustained in any group or organization.

Action is the distinguishing factor. Great leaders do not just have vision and purpose, communication skills and strategic thinking prowess. They act in ways that are consistent and aligned with their vision and messaging. This is how trust and followership is created. Leaders must be skilled at enrolling others to take action.

Excellence in leadership is governed by impeccable awareness and skillful alignment of integral relationships. Yoga of Leadership is the roadmap for leaders who want to master:

- Self-awareness; a powerful relationship with Self

- A sustainable and productive relationship with Time

- Effective communication and co-creation

- The power of intention; a vital relationship to Purpose

- Determination to promote positive change

This book is about leadership at its best. It is a shortcut to accessing the untapped potential of all organizations and leaders. It applies core yoga principles to help leaders get to the next level of excellence and to help organizations become more socially conscious bodies capable of profound world change.

This book is also about yoga, of course, so let's define it so we're on the same page there, too.

DEFINING YOGA:

yoga *n*

Yoga is a commonly known generic term for the physical, mental, and spiritual practices or disciplines which originated in ancient India with a view to attain a state of permanent peace.[1][2] Specifically, yoga is one of the six *āstika* ("orthodox") schools of Hindu philosophy. *Yoga Sūtras of Patañjali*, defines yoga as "the stilling of the changing states of the mind"[1]. Yoga has also been popularly defined as "union with the divine" in other contexts and traditions.[3] Wikipedia

Reflecting upon our aforementioned four A's of leadership, their yogic corollary would look like this:

Awareness: I know my conscious mind, intentions and aspirations ~and am clear on who I am and what I am doing. I seek truth, and understand the delusions that create pain and complexity. I understand "will" and ego and desire.

Authenticity: I strive to speak, see and listen from the heart.

Alignment: Knowledge and wisdom guide me. They inform every action with keen awareness.

Action: Every action is based upon clear intention and keen awareness.

What to Expect

Each chapter has a discussion section to introduce key ideas, and then a practice section with yoga poses, also known as postures or in Sanskrit, *asana*.

The asana section will be preceded by a brief analysis of three factors that influence each asana:

1. Core Leadership Concepts

2. Leadership Points of View

3. Yogic Points of View

These are to help guide intentions, create self-awareness, or engender a certain spirit when approaching each asana, intersecting and integrating leadership and yoga.

Each section will be followed by reflections, thoughts or ideas to enhance your experience "on the mat" or in your office or wherever you find yourself reading this book.

You will notice that this book is different from your average leadership or yoga book. First of all, it's shorter. We intended it to be concise and therefore appealing to the busy leaders for whom it's written. Second of all, we've bottom-lined it for you…we've stripped it of the usual anecdotes and stories and real life examples. This is intentional. Instead of stories, we give you practices and metaphors. You will author your own narrative as you ponder and apply the concepts we share here. Our examples are not relevant, for you will create your own, or you will recognize yourself and others you know as we describe the intersection of leadership and yoga. Therefore, this is not a business book, not a leadership book, not a yoga book, rather it is more a roadmap and guidebook, providing you with a framework upon which to build your own design. In it, you'll find concepts to ponder as well as actions you can take, so you can navigate in whatever manner suits you best.

What to Know

"What comes next, is the next breath." ~Linda Lang

Breathing is a fundamental of all yogic practice, and as such is tied to every action: a forward bend is associated with an exhalation, just as a strong standing position or back-bend is driven and inspired by the inhalation.

But more to our point, your ability to take a full breath is imperative for emotional stability and physiological balance, homeostasis and physical health, as well as alert mental functioning for problem solving, creativity and clear communication between your self and others.

This is EASY: Breathe in through the nose, out through the nose. Begin to feel the breath moving through your nostrils and throat, feel the chest expand. Breathe into the lower lungs, then let the breath rise toward the collar bones. Relax your belly and let it become round as you breathe in, and feel it contract when you breathe out.

This WILL take practice, and you WILL GET THIS and it will make all the difference in how you feel and what you do:

>Breath creates the space for keen awareness.
>
>It makes it possible for us to respond in the moment,
>
>rather than react based on past experience.
>
>It IS the difference between reacting and responding.
>
>THIS, is yoga.

Introduction: We begin

The Yoga of Leadership is the key that unlocks doorways to your own hidden strengths and limitless possibilities, that can remind all of us of how we can become exceptional in our lives: as leaders and followers, as friends, as family, as teachers and students, doctors and patients, as co-workers and policy-makers. It is where you will discover your inner resources of satisfaction, creativity, and fulfillment.

The Secret to Sanity in Insane Times

In this quick read, we reveal techniques that can calm down the driven, speed-addicted, efficiency-crazed, edgy, efficient-to-a-fault, multi-tasking, run-run-run executives we know and love. When leaders in this current Culture of Stress, bred from enhanced technologies, global competition and unpredictable market conditions, learn to embody practices from yogic traditions, there can be an immediate shift in awareness that leads to an enhanced sense of well-being.

This thinking enables leaders to achieve mastery over self-limiting behaviors and beliefs, through a personal transformation of their internal landscape that creates a mental shift, through physiological training, physical practice and psychological insight. This increased awareness, a mindfulness, makes explicit the parallels between yoga principles and exceptional leadership…a primer for the very successful, on the way up, or 'arrived' business Executive.

IN YOGA OF LEADERSHIP YOU WILL LEARN HOW TO:

- Find and manage time to your advantage
- Choose to respond to situations and feelings with centered calm, instead of reacting as usual
- Flip your switch from stress to self-awareness
- Move from unintended consequences of behavior, to legacy and intended impact
- Shift from chaos to clarity
- Train your mind towards inner calm, happiness, personal and organizational health — on demand
- Create harmony and balance using the most powerful antidotes to stress.

The format of this book is brief, inspirational lessons about the art and practice of yoga that have direct relevance to the art and practice of leadership. It's designed to be a pocket guide for motivation for those times when leaders feel stuck, unsure, knocked off balance, overwhelmed, or otherwise challenged.

Keep it in your office or briefcase for a quick idea, a short centering practice before a big meeting, or just a quick mental break to escape from your day. Flip it open as needed and find the answers to or about whatever's bugging you.

We don't aim to stretch leaders into pretzels and we are not here to urge you to stand on your head or bend over backwards… you already do that figuratively quite enough in order to meet the expectations of your boards, customers, media and stockholders!

We DO aim to entertain ideas that will stretch your mind, turn your world upside-down and find yourself head-over-heels about the beauty and simplicity of these ideas and their practical application into your busy daily life as a leader.

It's an exploration of self-expression, authenticity, and transparency in leadership, and it is for leaders at all levels of any organization. Great leaders have a congruency and awareness of their expression of themselves as leaders, meaning they have enormous alignment between their words and their use of body, tone, affect, emotional intelligence for the purpose of effective communication and influence. Some leaders are naturally charismatic, others are powerful because of their ability to align their core self with their outward expression and create environments of trust and safety. On the flip side, those leaders who drive people crazy are the ones who demonstrate incongruence between their words and their expression (body and tone), thus creating mixed messages to their people, to the media, to the board, to the stakeholders, to the customers, etc.

Anxiety, malaise and even depression often run rampant among leaders, who have little or no time for reflection and processing. Our leaders experience the same 'burn-out' many of their too-pressed employees complain about. *How do today's executive leaders re-charge, calm busy minds, protect time and space for reflection and meditation-- not to mention creative thought?* Does leadership take more 'down time'? Doesn't creating vision and strategy, a leader's main job -- require space? We see that there are significant ways of approaching time, thought, the mind and body connections that can be ultimately valuable to the practice of leadership provided by yoga whether a leader takes it on as a practice or not. Yoga is access to creating more space.

Yoga is a practice that allows leaders the ultimate in leadership mastery: the ability to train their mind for inner freedom, happiness, and peace. Yoga impacts the body chemistry at the level of experience and at the source of the pain; it balances the nervous system. So much of leadership is about the BEING of a leader, and yoga is one path to access mastery in being able to BE. **So, this inner freedom coupled with the ability to be a pure leader brings wisdom, peace, neutrality and compassion to the bottom line business results of any organization. It is the next level of leadership that our global businesses crave.**

Yoga gives access to the deepest sense of self-expression. Learning that congruence between body and self through yoga can actually make you, as a leader, more articulate in your communication style. You gain awareness of your own congruency between your emotions and your body. For instance, when a yoga teacher says "just stand up" when you have your leg twisted around your shoulder and you are upside down looking behind yourself, you push through doubts, anxiety, fear, limiting beliefs, and — seemingly miraculously — just stand up. That expression of self is very powerful. It is one of the discoveries that keeps people in yoga; they find a new avenue for this congruency of self expression. As a yoga student and as a leader you have to work at it. It feels uncomfortable at first, your body may not articulate the way others do around you. However, the moment at which you connect your vision (what you see yourself doing) to your emotional space, your body (or organization) cooperates, it all comes through. It is a perfect expression of self. You can feel it when you've got everything lined up, clicked into place, and it is all in sync. There's an ease and effortlessness that comes at that moment. New space is created, and a lightness and joy and certain peace is achieved. We've seen it in yoga and we've seen it when a team comes together in shared leadership towards a common vision or goal in an organization.

The Bottom Line

As leaders, when we don't see ourselves perform, we get feedback from others, from data, from media, from consumers. Yoga (and masterful leadership) is about *self*-feedback, *insight*.

Yoga teaches how to survive and thrive in an increasingly complex world. The yoga postures and breathing, if done correctly and regularly, actually calm and balance our nervous system. Some can be applied in everyday commerce, moment to moment, in the regular course of a leader's day.

Using the powerful simple tool of awareness to access the difference between good leaders and exceptional leaders will allow you to get in control of your behaviors, increase your freedom of self expression and positively improve your impact on others. The tool of awareness is the secret to the way we impact others. Everything comes from it: motivation, leading others, mastering yourself, making a difference, resolving breakdowns, getting results.

There are many books about leadership, why write another one? What can yoga possibly offer leaders? To the casual observer, the comparison might seem strange – even remote. In many ways, the practice of yoga provides a wonderful metaphor for leadership. One could argue that leadership is about achievement, about winning, and about money, whereas yoga is nothing about such worldly goals of capitalism. You'd be right. However, in order to "succeed" in yoga, which we realize is a very Western way of thinking, one must master certain basic intrinsic and universal principles that require thought, learning and practice. The very elements of being that one must master in yoga are profoundly powerful as key tools for success in leadership. Our assertion in this book is that the BEING of a masterful leader is wholly aligned with the being required of yoga practitioners.

Yoga is about being present in the moment, being in the now, creating space, breathing and centering, stretching and balance. Any powerful leader will tell you that personal mastery as a foundation for leadership also comes from these very principles. Stephen Covey calls it "sharpening the saw", Peter Senge calls it "Personal Mastery". Both yoga and leadership require engagement. One must practice the core elements of both in order to grow, to learn, to expand one's capacity, to succeed. Simple observation of leadership does not make one a strong leader, neither does watching someone do yoga make one a more grounded, spiritual master.

We invite managers, executives, businesspeople, leaders, the casual observer and the serious student of leadership to explore some of the most basic principles of yoga as a practical metaphor for leadership. The principles are guides, one must be in the practice to learn. The fundamental purpose of this book is to share the metaphor and charge you with identifying what you can apply to your business and how.

We realized in our respective yoga practices that the masterful leadership and guidance from our yoga instructors that inform our yoga practice, that allow us to play our edge, to create yoga poses from the inside-out, and breathe space into our bodies to allow for new expansion are also great words of wisdom for leaders of all kinds when applied to the challenging, often solitary practice of leadership.

Soften your awareness.
Embrace stillness.
Breathe fully, with deep breath in, and a longer exhalation.

These skills are counter-intuitive to modern leaders who had to drive to get to the top.

THIS is what's missing to get leaders to the next level, to get organizations to be socially conscious bodies capable of profound world change. This is about results, about leadership at its best, and about accessing untapped potential: ours and others.

Chapter 1
Executive Presence:
The Outer Expression of Inner Intention

"True leadership is a fire in the mind that transforms all who feel its warmth, that transfixes all who see its shining light in the eyes of a man or a woman.

It is a strength of purpose and belief in a cause that reaches out to others, touches their hearts and makes them eager to follow."
— Secretary of Defense Robert M. Gates
US Naval Academy Commencement May 27, 2011

LEADERSHIP starts with a vision, or as Gates says, "the fire in the mind" driven by a keen awareness of "purpose and belief" followed by conscious action "that transforms."

This is how an exceptional leader touches the minds of others.

YOGA is a practice that allows leaders the ultimate in leadership mastery: the ability to train the mind for passionate creativity, meaningful inquiry and mindful engagement that leads to charismatic presence, unflappable confidence and the ability to inspire others.

We offer an integral approach to leadership; integrating body and spirit with the mind of the leader.

Innovative Influence and Transformational Relationships

This is the goal of modern visionary leadership: to appeal to the minds of stakeholders, to convince them of the positive change required for future success, to win them over. Once an individual becomes a follower and embraces the idea, they become a partner in the emerging change, a co-creator. Innovative influence is that place where awareness, authenticity, and aligned action intersect to shift and transform relationships. The best leaders are masters of this innovative influence.

Innovative influence is the secret to the magic that happens when it all works: the recognition of who we are and what is really happening; an awareness, through inquiry, of the energy at play, allowing ourselves to see the relationship between inner and outer awareness, to see the relationship between inner realities and external realities, and to comprehend the relationship between you and me and everyone else. It is more than the state of being that allows you to approach problem solving, it is being in relationship WITH the problem to be solved. It is being in relationship with the possible future created by the solution. It is the ability to see the simplicity within the complexity of all the moving parts.

Leadership, like yoga, is ultimately a solitary pursuit, often in the company of others. In both cases, breakthroughs are hard won yet occur as exquisitely simple insights, rewarding us with a deeper awareness of our innermost intentions, our heart's desires. Both pursuits create a greater possibility for deeper, more meaningful relationships.

It's not just about transformational relationships with peers, or supervisors, clients or direct reports. Yoga of Leadership is the ability to create transformational relationships with all the facets of yourself and the circumstances in which you find yourself required to lead.

The Total Expression of Self: Executive Presence

Leadership strength comes from an authentic and aligned expression of self. Yoga gives us access to our deepest sense of self-expression. Congruency between body and self through yoga can actually make you, as a leader, more articulate and clear in your communication style. As a leader, when you express yourself and your leadership point of view fully, you open new doors in your leadership capacity, thus setting in motion the opportunities for greater results.

Yoga begins with an idea, a thought that impacts body chemistry at the level of experience; it balances the nervous system. There is a moment at which you connect your vision (what you see yourself doing) to your emotional space -- your body (or organization) cooperates. It is a perfect expression of self. You can feel it when you've got everything lined up, clicked into place, and it is all in sync. There's an ease and effortlessness that comes at that moment. A refined sense of space is created, and a lightness, joy and certain peace is achieved. We've seen it in yoga and we've seen it when a team comes together in shared leadership towards a common vision or shared goal in an organization.

How you appear as a leader is often referred to as executive presence. This includes many factors and variables, from your attitude, beliefs, image, brand, language, eye contact and attire, to your political savvy, gravitas, situational awareness, interpersonal skills, emotional intelligence, strategic prowess, and presentation skills.

You can have amazing executive presence even if you lack charisma.

Introverts can have strong executive presence.

Entry-level professionals and manual laborers can have executive presence.

Embedded in it is the concept of being fully present.

When you are fully present, you are focused in the moment, clear, grounded, and aligned with that which matters in any given context. Your presence is present as a conscious and intentional act. Think of it this way:

> executive presence = a fully conscious being is present

The manner in which you stand and move, the various ways you approach customers, co-workers, support personnel, supervisors, bosses, executive staff or Board of Directors conveys a great deal about how you feel about yourself as an individual and in relationship to others. Bill Clinton and Oprah Winfrey have both been described by folks who meet them for the first time as making each person they are with feel like the only person in the room. It's that quality of conscious presence that leaves people who interact with them feeling special, seen, and valued.

Your position, both political and professional, and your attitude are frequently expressed by your posture and facial expressions, possibly to your disadvantage. The strength of your leadership style will be enhanced by developing a profound understanding of who you are, behind the stories you customarily tell and believe about yourself. Your executive presence is your ability to convey physically, energetically, and through words that which you wish to communicate. When your executive presence is aligned with your intended leadership brand, others see the leader you'd like to be known as, which may be different from the assumptions and perceptions they've attributed to the leader you are. Your Executive Presence, like your personal brand, is essentially the story about you that enters the room before you do. What is it that people know to be true about you (or assume and agree is true about you) that may or may not be what you intended? Everyone has a personal brand, whether you've ever been aware of it or not. In many cases it's an unconscious, automatic brand…the cumulation of others' collective and individual experiences of how you show up over time. Your ability to bring your presence consciously into your executive presence will allow alignment to emerge between your brand and how you'd like to be known by others.

So, how do you access the type of presence we describe? So glad you asked!

The first Yoga of Leadership pose we'd like to share with you is one that gives you access to that truly present executive presence detailed above, and can be used as either a metaphor or a practice.

ASANA #1: TADASANA (Mountain Pose)

"Ta-Da!"

Stand Tall, like a mountain or skyscraper, and imagine endless sky behind you.

Arms rest by your side, chest is broad and held high, feet are firmly planted, just hip-width apart. Breathe.

In mountain pose, we dedicate ourselves to a quality of mind that provides the optimal environment for balanced awareness and creative problem solving. Mountain pose is known as *tadasana*.

A mountain is a sentinel, dominant on the horizon. It is a landmark, a point of reference. It can be a Mt. Sinai, St. Helen's or Mount Everest. It can be volcanic and explosive, accessible or inaccessible. It's either a bleak wilderness or rich habitat.

The Sanskrit definition of *tada*, is strong, like a mountain; loaded with metaphors of strength, endurance, trustworthiness and enduring presence. *Tada* is solid, reliable, permanent. It is majestic, powerful yet humble. *Tada* is essentially grounded, rooted in what is Real.

Asana is an action infused with the breath.

As a yoga posture, *tadasana* is simply one person standing tall, being still, breathing, alert, awake and fully aware. Visible, composed, inwardly focused.

As a leadership posture, it's a quiet calm, a grounded yet confident stance. A solid foundation from which to lead and speak.

Another name for this primary posture is *Samasthitihi*: *sama* is equality and harmony, aligned and straight, honorable and fully present; *sthitihi* connotes a supreme quality of stillness.

Try It Yourself!

Stand Tall, like a mountain or skyscraper, and imagine endless sky behind you.

Arms rest by your side, chest is broad and held high, feet are firmly planted, just hip-width apart. Breathe.

You convey reassurance and strength, fully in your body, uplifted while grounded and balanced.

Your eyes are bright and clear, your comportment is noble, your mood is contagious.

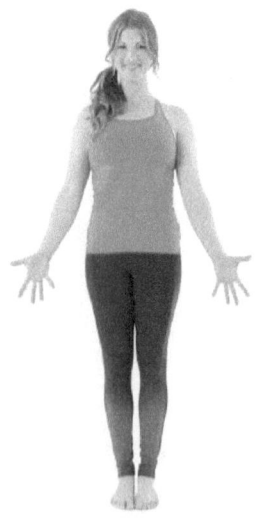

RICK CUMMINGS

You are an icon of elegance and serenity: present, confident, influential, charismatic, inspirational and filled with potential that wants to be shared.

A magnetic force flows through you, informed by your strength of purpose and belief in your Self, as well as what you intend to achieve.

You are compelling. You embody grace, and dignity and honor.

You are capable of observing yourself from the inside out: your breath, your posture, your connection to reality, your presence in the landscape, your prominence, your perspective.

At some point in time, you begin to feel, to realize that you are in a position of leadership, that others are looking to you for a sense of direction, a sense of purpose, a sense of belonging.

But first, you must BE capable of observing your Self, quiet and still. Simply present.

This requires profound stillness, turning awareness inward in order to recognize the nature of positive change from within and find the flow of energy in highly personal terms. If what you sense is not congruent with "positive" change and is no longer effective, efficient or appropriate, it needs to be converted, rejected or left behind. This must be achieved before an individual can begin to master leadership of others…Inquire. Be still. Breathe.

In mountain pose, we dedicate ourselves to a quality of mind that provides the optimal environment for balanced awareness and creative problem solving.

Core Leadership Concepts:

- Access to Executive Presence, and recognition of that presence as a force

- Visible, Magnetic, Compelling, somehow irresistible

- Source of Trust & Inspiration

- Time-honored, a survivor

- Being seen and known

Leadership Points of View:

- Stand your ground,

- Walk your Talk

- Confident, Accessible, Steadfast

- Let your presence speak for you

- Simplicity and patience are honorable attributes

- • Be the sentinel

Yogic Points of View:

- Grounded, yet up-lifted, "Feet rooted to the ground, head in the clouds"

  - An *Ayurvedic dosha* is a primary quality: kapha is earth and water; pitta is fire; vata is wind, movement and flow.

- Feet firmly rooted is a condition of connection, head in the clouds alludes to the creativity and visionary properties of vata.

- *Yin* Practice: contemplative, awake and aware with the quality of timelessness

- *Bhavana*: Intentionality, feeling and knowing what you stand for with a sense of devotion and dedication to the highest ideals

How to Practice Mountain Pose:

We begin with breathing: A primary mantra, or phrase, perhaps: *so hahm, hahm sa*. In Sanskrit, it refers to the flow of every breath, the natural sound of simply breathing in and out. A little sizzle of "*so hahm*" breathing out, the "ah" of *hahm sa*, breathing in. It means, *I am this, this I am...*

Stand tall, feel your feet firmly rooted in all that you believe, all that you know and trust. Sense confidence rising up from this foundation and open to the possibilities that arise from that place of knowing.

Arms rest by your side with a current of energy that tones the muscles and hugs them to the bones. Palms roll outward (supinate) which invites the arm bones to roll up and back, the humerus slides beneath the shoulder blade and toward the spine, and moves the rib cage forward and upward. Keep the side body long, inner body bright...the back body undulates, tailbone drops toward the ground, like an anchor.

Create and connect to this firm foundation, breathe into a sense of center and stability to create an attitude of "I DO know what

I am doing." Be self-assured, self-knowing; notice how you convey this through your posture and demeanor.

Breathe in deeply, pause at the top, and then release the breath with a slow and gentle flow, and pause again at the bottom of the exhalation. Continue this simple breathing pattern as you reach your arms to the side, as if to say, "Here I Am."

Hold your head high, lift your chest and be bold. Remain still, yet alert. Own your power.

The first great lesson is finding your ground, your comfort zone, and knowing where YOU stand: confidence in the truest sense of the word.

When you can cultivate an inner awareness of this foundation, you can truly relax, thus increasing your ability to think clearly and set up better actions. When you are in public, it is the patience and calmness you convey, that makes others comfortable and confident in YOU.

Breathe in comfort, turn your breath into comfort, harness comfort as you harness your breath. Breath is comfort. Remember this.

Now, extend your arms to the sky, gazing toward the sun as if to say "Here I am," then slowly bring your hands to the heart in prayer position and with humility, honor your essence, that bright inner light of inspiration and encouragement.

Dare to be luminary.

It is this light, the light of your innermost being, which illuminates your quest to shape the future with wisdom and awareness. It is that which endows your vision with realistic expectations. It is also the light that draws attention to your ideas and attracts followers. It is this light that attracts others to your sense of purpose, and leads to transformation and followership.

Reflections: Self-Observation, Self-awareness

As you observe yourself in yoga, as well as in leadership positions, you have to be a self-observer; watching your Self, your being, your consciousness, in addition to your body and your mind. One of the things to observe in addition to your thoughts, is your feelings. Observe yourself with grace.

A leader's primary job is to build on the present to create the future, to breathe new life into an organization. It is the task of a leader to speak of the future in a way that makes that specific Future possible, to bring life to it so that people are able to respond in accordance with that future, their actions are aligned and consistent with that future. If sufficiently enrolled, people will not only embrace the declared future, but it will become a shared future and people will take engaged actions that align with manifesting that shared future. The leader creates a future within which the followers can see themselves and step into empowered action. The leader creates the space within which results happen.

Leadership, like yoga, is a thoughtful, considered series of actions consistent with an envisioned future; it is both visionary and expansive.

Actions, both yogic and logistic, must arise from a clear understanding of present conditions, a reliable and time-tested ground upon which change can occur. Deep, gentle breathing creates clarity of mind.

A yoga practitioner builds upon basic poses that are created by and with the breath. Each breath leads to the next breath as the physical actions of the body unfold. Increasingly challenging postures can be entertained, but only after having mastered the basics of balanced awareness physically and mentally, having a clear intention and maintaining calm control. The first posture (*tadasana*) IS this, it arises from the first breath in, and reveals the luminous simplicity of the mind.

Balanced Awareness: The Ability to Organize Action from Within

In yoga, first, we focus inside, with awareness focused on sensations so frequently skipped in the speed and fractious quality of daily life. We seek, and intentionally feel those internal physical sensations; the muscles stretching, the tendons pulling and moving closer to the bone, we also intentionally feel those physical sensations that translate into emotions. We create movement from a place of knowing, fully aware. So that which we become within a pose, evolves from our inner intention, is reflected in the outer expression of that pose, as a transformation.

Leadership similarly requires a balanced awareness and ability to organize from within, although rather than muscles and tendons and bone, it's about resources and systems and internal political nuances. Leaders create movement from a place of knowing, fully aware, that evolves from an inner intention and reflects external transformation in the form of results.

Timing: The first look at Patience

"So when I stand in mountain pose, how long should I be there? How do I know when to move or transition to the next pose?" Mountain pose is an exercise in humility; it is, by nature, a simple posture that can reveal the most complex aspects of the practice. To learn true patience and develop equanimity, practice patience here, noting that what comes next is only the next breath.

You might ask yourself, "What is my relationship with Time?" In your work as a leader, how do you identify the right moment to act, when to observe, when to wait? How do you find patience within your self, and how do you encourage others to use time to their advantage without acting prematurely or failing to know when the time is right?

Practice stillness. Be still and Know.

Chapter Two
Executive Insight
The Art of Balanced Awareness:
Inner Intention and Being the "I" of the Storm

We invite you to remember the gentleness of the breath as you step out of a posture of stability and into what comes next, into the unknown. This breath creates the "relaxation response" identified by Dr. Herbert Benson of Harvard University, and is simply an inhalation followed by a longer exhalation. It creates a reaction in the sympathetic nervous system that says "I am safe." And voila ~ your blood pressure is reduced, your heart rate slows down. There is patience where there was anger, and insight where there was confusion.

I am breathing, I am the breath.

So ham, ham sa...

Remember this. And continue...knowing that what comes next, is the next breath.

In the last chapter we discussed the practice of executive presence in a quiet, controlled posture. Both feet on the ground. But once we step into a role of leadership, the ground can become unsteady, attitudes shift like heavy winds, and a sense of stability and control can become one of vulnerability and dread. A core leadership skill is that of finding stability regardless of the circumstances around you.

When batted about by life and the winds of fortune, YOU are the one who must stay centered and grounded. Where we live, the earth is solid; but elsewhere it has a tendency to shake and quake and explode, unpredictably. Now isn't that an interesting symbol for the economy, for fiscal certainty, for personal and professional security? This unpredictability creates ANXIETY, which is a destabilizing force. So if we return to the motto of "just Breathe" it may seem easier said than done, right? The military has a term for the state of the global climate today which also applies to most organizations: VUCA, which stands for Volatility, Uncertainty, Complexity, and Ambiguity. Leaders must lead in these VUCA conditions, and increasingly, these are not temporary states, rather it is becoming the new normal.

It is one thing to find the patience and presence to stand tall, alert and aware for extended periods of time (like waiting a really long time for economic indicators to change, or waiting for your strategic plan to evolve and transform), but it is something else entirely to learn to balance without the supports to which you have become accustomed.

The second yoga of leadership pose we present is one that allows you to access a state of steady balance regardless of external factors. Balance is generated from within.

ASANA #2: *VRKSASANA* (Tree Pose)

Tree Pose: Stand boldly, on one leg. That's all.

Directions: Stand on one leg. Really. For a long time. We'll teach you how.

Envision a solitary tree, in a very windy place; or yourself, a lone voice with what feels like the weight of the world on your shoulders. Or perhaps return your awareness to the Gates quote at the beginning of the book, and envision yourself as a leader with ideas that ignite the "fire in the mind that transforms all who feel its warmth, that transfixes all who see its shining light."

Simply visualize yourself:

A Woman In High Heels Or Man In Wing Tips

She slips off her shoes and her jacket ~ He removes the shoes, jacket and loosens his tie.

Or perhaps more appropriately for you,

A Woman in Birkenstocks or a Man in Sandals

She on a rock overlooking the creek, he at the sea...

You in this posture:

Stand Tall, begin in Mountain Pose

Core Leadership Concepts:

• Expertise and confidence

• Security and Protection

• Ability to join the ranks, get your hands dirty, dig in

Leadership Points of View:

• Total commitment • Responsiveness

• Resilience

• Flexibility

- Balance

Yogic Points of View:

- *Santosha*, acceptance of What Is, satisfaction, equipoise

- *Tapas*, perseverance and dedication

- *Bhavana*, a feeling of belonging and deep connection

How to practice Tree Pose:

Stand tall in Mountain pose, shift your weight to the right leg.

Root down strongly with your right leg, and place the left foot against your right shin or thigh; root the left foot into the standing right leg.

Hands are in the *namaste position, pressed together with thumbs towards your heart and fingertips pointing upwards. This position is called anjali mudra.* Breathe gently, lift up through the crown of your head. If unsteady, reclaim your balance and reconnect as instructed above.

In yoga, a *mudra* is the outer expression of an inner intention; the most well known example would be hands facing each other with palms pressed together in prayer position; *anjali mudra*. A comparable business *mudra* communicates confidence and trustworthiness; relationships begin, connections are made, and deals are sealed with a firm handshake in the professional world.

Breathe. Relax into the balance on your right leg. If you are so inclined, you can stretch your arms up and reach out the "branches" of your "tree" to expand your expression. Or you can stay balanced with your hands in the prayer position. Close your eyes and breathe.

Repeat using the opposite leg. Breathe.

Reflections: Creating Stability through Strength

If you are the eye, or in our case the "I" of the Storm, you are at the center of uncontrollable forces of nature. Indeed, people who take on leadership positions can truly identify with this concept! Breath work is the calming influence, the Blue Sky above and within, the source of steadiness and focus on what is happening moment to moment.

Align the body with thoughtful awareness of the desire to create stability through strength.

Using the principles of gentle breath, alignment, and understanding the flow of energy allows yoga students to acquire stability and lightness at will. Powerful leaders also cultivate this ability to self-generate stability and lightness regardless of chaos and drama around them.

An attitude of lightness and play, a mastery of the principles of alignment and the breath, creates action. Breathing, being grounded and rooting energetically down into the earth (envisioning earth as a solid foundation) allows us to expand the action (rise up or reach out) and create space for more, for greater results. There is a movement between grounding, expanding, acting, relaxing and getting centered again. And that movement is uplifting and enlivening: transfixing, transformative.

Doesn't your role as a leader often feel like you're trying to get everything done while balancing on one foot? Leaders who lack awareness of how to create a strong balanced platform from their one rooted leg often find themselves swayed by political influences (internal, national, and global) and market volatility; they are reactive rather than guiding the organization from an intentional place. Tree pose is a practice that, once mastered can be applied to any leadership scenario.

As a leader you will be able to bring awareness to what is needed to set up balance, sustain balance, or regain balance if it wavers. Your body is a metaphor for your team, organization, or community (depending on what you lead). It's the same awareness skill, applied in a different context.

Slow Down to Speed Up, Root Down to Rise Up, and other Paradoxes of Leadership

Yoga calls for being in the space between paradoxes. It is not uncommon to hear a yoga instructor direct the class to "root down in order to rise up". Grounding the body into the earth in order to reach for higher possibilities, to stretch out of the ribcage and reach with delight into the unknown. As leaders, we must keep our people and our organizations grounded in numbers, firmly footed in a strong foundation in order to pursue lofty ideals or grand visions. New product development, R&D, marketing life cycles all depend on this same yoga principle of rooting down in order to rise up. Think about crisis situations or how a leader must handle the media in a situation where something when wrong. If the leader is not grounded in strong organizational history, branding, values, and results, it will be hard to improve, if not create new public perception. Leaders often deal in the currency of paradox. They have to make tough choices and unpopular decisions as well as motivate, inspire, and draw out the best from others. Where are you, as a leader, not embracing opposites or paradoxes that would make a difference in the results you are trying to produce? Where are you resisting opposing forces and creating obstacles for yourself, your people, or your organization?

The Mythic Quest for Control

For every student of yoga there are two watershed moments. The first is where you catch yourself falling clumsily out of a balance pose and think "it's okay to fall". The second is when the body settles into the same pose without effort and with inspiring stability. Neither state generated by force of will; both are bookends of discovery. Finding and maintaining control in challenging positions is a mythic yogic quest. Balancing postures give us experiences on the mat with seeking security and sustaining it, losing it and reclaiming it. Where do you have control? Where do you lose control? In the beginning, we choose to stay with safety. Stay with comfort. Stay with foundational elements. Stay with what you know. Stay with what feels good. Regain balance by returning to the fundamentals. These are important instructions for yoga, which translate to wisdom for leading in difficult situations. When you are feeling unstable, unsure, or otherwise not entirely balanced, generating and claiming an intention of control, comfort, safety, and knowing, helps regain the footing to discover what works. This inward intention is mirrored by the outward expression of those leadership qualities.

Being able to return to that place of comfort instills confidence with a new awareness; this is the key. In business we sometimes call it regrouping – going back to the basics. But yoga teaches it not as a retreat but as finding solid footing to begin the next posture.

TRANSITIONAL ASANA:
UTTANASANA (Intense Stretch/Forward Bend)

Bend at the waist, bow into Uttansana, a standing forward bend, with your head to your knees.

Repeat *Tadasana (Mountain pose)* once more, a tall and uplifting posture that communicates PRESENCE, reassurance, trustworthiness and dedication.

Roll your arms until you feel the arm bones (humeri) rotating in the shoulder socket. Feel how your chest lifts higher as the palms roll up, and as they roll down, bend at the waistline and take a bow. Repeat several times peacefully along with your inhale and exhale, imagining you can hear the crowd cheer.

This pose is called *Uttanasana*, it is an intense forward bend. It is a pose of honoring one's self, of reverence and humility. It reminds us of our true nature as a source of light and luminosity. This light is the emission that transfixes, captures peoples' attention and ignites imaginations, creates followers, engages colleagues and inspires co-creators.

The posture is an inversion since the head is below the heart; it can be practiced sitting or standing to relieve tightness and tension, to clear your head, to remove cobwebs from between your ears. Inversions are like mental-floss, or like a cerebral oil change. When your head hangs down, give it a little shake to release some of the nonsense that has been accumulating in there!

When dealt a blow in business or in leadership, standing forward bend can help you reclaim your ability to think clearly, releasing the emotion and drama and energy drain of whatever broadsided you and allow you to remember your strength.

MICHAEL WINOKUR

Chapter Three
From Individual Awareness, to Global Perspective

What comes next, is the next breath...

Breathing change into other individuals, situations and organizations

Leadership is the ability to stand, like a sentinel, on the uncertain shoreline of the future as a source of stability, reliability and enlightened awareness.

When uncertainty arises, we often unconsciously stop breathing. At this point, we recommend taking a deep inhale and deeper exhale, at which point you will discover a new energy to move (peacefully) to the next pose. In the business world, it is comparable to removing ourselves from a discouraging situation and gliding into the next moment with ease. This requires vision, perspective ~ a sense of knowing where we are.

ASANA #4: *Garudasana* - Eagle Pose

Envision: An eagle standing on the highest point of a pine tree. An admiral standing on the deck of an aircraft carrier. The President, facing the nation. You, sitting on a rocky ledge overlooking the sea. Each is surveying the territory, the landscape...the outside world, from within the inner world; the realms of external engagement, and inner awareness.

Core Leadership Concepts:

- Uber-responsibility

- Micro/macro Vision
- ACTION, TIMING, WISDOM

Leadership Points of View:

- Eagle's View IS 360 degree Perspective
- Sense of Direction, Fearlessness
- Increasing the capacity of your people to see new futures
- FOCUS, KNOWING the BIG PICTURE and fully aware of the details without
- becoming involved in the minutia or limited by the details.

Yogic Points of View:

- Control, balance, expansive focus, unlimited freedom
- Noble and wise, known for prowess
- Speed and spontaneity, explosive force
- Patient and deft

How to practice Eagle Pose:

Try this first sitting in your chair. Sit tall, find a sense of center and tone the muscles in your legs as you cross your right leg over the left, tucking your right foot behind your left calf if possible. Now wrap/twist/interlace your arms in front of your face, bent at the elbows, fingers upward -- keep them strong. Hug your legs together. Sit as tall as you can and breathe gently and deeply.

You will feel some constriction, and that's normal, just breathe into the back of your body where it feels open and stretched. Soften your gaze, and breathe into this posture. Keep your arms and fingers charged with energy.

The eagle has 360-degree vision, knows the landscape, can see the entire picture and scan from one field of view to the other. The eagle also has refined visual acuity and depth of vision, can see the smallest movement on the forest floor.

A leader with eagle vision knows the big picture and the fine detail, senses nuances and shifts, has an uncanny sense of timing and the ability to expose obstacles in order to achieve the goal.

Now, try *garudasana* standing. Center yourself, hug in (meaning imagine your muscles hugging the bones in your legs/arms, knit your ribs together), cross the right leg over the left, and breathe. Find balance and stability. Feel free to spread your "wings" as you lift and lower your arms. Now wrap/twist/interlace your arms in front of you, bent at the elbows, fingers upward -- keep them strong. Hug your legs together. Stand as tall as you can and breathe gently and deeply.

Then, once you feel balanced, try to lift the toes of the right foot, and there you will find balance AND perspective. Breathe into the fullness of this possibility.

Eagle pose is a posture that requires the patience developed in a long-held Mountain Pose, with the ability to learn how to balance in what first feels quite precarious and vulnerable, but with patience and perseverance, becomes just a part of the practice. We learn to embrace our vulnerability and use it to our advantage, even if it creates discomfort. We find stability and ease in a position that can otherwise create tension and over-efforting.

Reflections:

Lead, and Practice, from Your Heart

Yoga instructors say, "Soften the heart, open the heart, lead from the heart" to help us melt into a pose and remind us to breathe more and effort less. It is a reminder to relax into it, to breathe into it, rather than focus on the performance indicators of success. It is a gentle nudge to tap into the heart energy rather than staying in our heads, where we are analyzing the best next move. Leaders are good at the head stuff. We have MBAs and experience to draw on. We have superb analytical skills and the capacity for (if not time for) strategic thought. We have vision and mission and goals. We also have another thing that lives in the head: fear. Leaders have fear. Many leaders are terrified that if we stop the drive, it will all fall apart. Leading from the heart requires facing that fear, and getting out of the head space of solving, analyzing, synthesizing and logic-ing one's way to the ideal state. In yoga, you can't think your way into a pose. You can try, but the sublime lightness and energy that comes with the purest expression of the pose comes from the heart, from the breath, and from someplace entirely outside of one's head. There is no fear there. When a yoga student fears falling, that is the precise moment when balance is lost. So, too, with a leader who has not faced his or her fears. Vulnerability can be a powerful tool of leadership, when handled with maturity and gravitas.

FEAR, Balanced Awareness, Keen Awareness

In Eagle Pose, we feel the "fear" of standing, from expansive and open to contracted and tight, from a balanced and grounded position into a one-legged balance as if we are perched upon the highest branches of a tree. We observe and thus experience that tingling and tightening in the chest as our mind says, "I can't possibly do this" while we do stand strong. We feel that fear morphing into the expelled breath of elation! Such emotions, when noticed by the observer-mind as physical sensations, allow again for choice versus characteristic reaction, and cease to become barriers to new positions, new ideas, and new growth!

Fear is the barrier that stops the risk necessary for growth. Great leaders know that they must find courage and help their people to find the courage to risk. Leaders are not absent of fear. They have the skill to know and experience their fear and move out from fear to courage, just as in yoga we build the pose from the inside out. Yoga, like leadership, is an "inside out proposition", meaning the internal state moves the action and the position of the body is generated from the internal expression and alignment of muscle energy, breath, and intention. It is not unusual to try over and over to do a move in yoga, see that you don't have the strength, then two months later find yourself doing it with ease.

Chapter Four
Leadership as an exercise in Perspective & Preparedness

A successful leader needs a precise understanding of the circumstances and forces at play in the world around him. He needs to be believable, reliable and capable. He needs to be capable of full engagement in the process of a leadership challenge, effective and knowledgeable of the territory in which he operates. That knowledge arises from a relationship that grows between inner awareness and a reliable perception of external realities: a synthesis that becomes a defensible perspective of what is true.

In order to accurately perceive the external territory, any leader must first have a clear understanding of who he is as an individual, be able to define his commitments and beliefs ~ both personally and in relationship to the world around him; more specifically, the world in which he wishes to lead others toward positive change. Only then can he step with confidence into that territory to create the conversation within a community to fully ascertain what is true and emerging, to have a trustworthy perspective and the ability to know for what to be prepared. It is this ability to listen to the employees, the other leaders, the community at large that allows a strong leader to realistically assess the landscape and clearly see the current trends and coming future.

To achieve such balanced awareness, one must draw upon certain tools of the trade. In yoga those tools are discernment, single pointed focus, patience and steadfastness. The yogi is mindful and intentional, contemplative yet strident, gentle while forceful. The actions are responsive and reflective rather than reactive and knee-jerk. These tools would serve leaders well.

In the yoga practice, before one fully executes a pose, there is a great deal of time spent creating a foundation with firm footing. Similarly, someone in a leadership position would want to work in an arena where they have meaningful experience and expertise.

It is the process of preparing, of setting up the pose, that is as meaningful as the action itself. There is a profound relationship between the desire to act, the knowledge of how to act, and finally a readiness for the action.

Asana #5: *Virbhadrasana*, Warrior Pose I

Envision an archer standing alone, with a field of targets in the distance. Imagine the bow, a quiver of arrows, a certain attainment of skill. She's fully prepared. A deer walks across the path...

Envision holding a leadership position, standing in front of a room of shareholders, facts and figures in hand, computer presentation ready, strategic plan highlighted, tasks delineated, jobs delegated. An opportunity arises...

Core Leadership Concepts:

- Connection and Commitment

- Embodiment

- Stability, Timing, Steadfastness, Fearlessness, Control

- The strength of purpose, conviction and commitment, are palpable.

Leadership Points of View:

- Patience

- Stability and Control

- Preparedness

- Know what you stand for: Be Seen and Be Known

Yogic Points of View:

- *Tapas*, tenacity

- Self-knowing and the Guru Principle: we learn to listen to, and trust, our inner voice

- Discernment and discrimination, seeing clearly

How to practice Warrior I:

Stand tall in mountain pose, then step your feet wide apart. Lift your arms out to the sides.

Tone the muscles in your arms and legs until you look (and feel) like a five pointed star.

MICHAEL WINOKUR

Imagine yourself star-like, luminous, like a beacon, a lighthouse, with the ability to transfix: sense the potentiality of this expression of strength and public persona, then draw your awareness inward to find the breath, to fill with light from the inside out.

This is leadership, the ability to stand on the uncertain shoreline of the future as a source of stability, reliability and enlightened awareness. You have the capacity to do this.

Now turn your feet 90 degrees towards the right or left (whichever direction you define as forward), both in the same direction and firmly grounded in your foundation, hips squared. Bend your right leg to 90 degrees, reach your arms forward in the same direction your feet are pointing and then swing them to the sky, as if energy was radiating out from the center of your being.

You are like the bow of an archer, a warrior in pursuit of a better world. You open your body, lift your heart and gently, boldly gaze into the future. You embody the tools you need to see clearly, both where you stand and that for which you stand.

You breathe, again and again.

Keep your eyes on the prize; keep the target in focus, whether it's a performance metric or a target market. Or as in yoga, the heart is always the target, compassion and unconditional acceptance the prize.

Your front leg is at a right angle, your thigh begins to whisper, "I'm getting tired." You hold the pose for many more breaths, shifting your awareness to the strength rising from the foundation in the back foot. (Or, you have been waiting a very long time for positive results, and the nature of change is SO

SLOW; you crave conditions that are optimal for evolution and transformation to occur, but the flow is obstructed, results are delayed.)

Leader as warrior is not a new concept, however the pose of warrior reminds leaders to expand our reach, widening our horizons and growing beyond stale limitations.

Reflections:

Finding the Edge of Comfort

The edge of personal comfort is not merely that place between simple discomfort and ragged pain. The edge is like a shoreline that expands and contracts; energy and desire are the tides.

We expand the shoreline of our comfort by allowing energy to flow away from the center, expanding the possibilities.

Is our level of comfort limiting us, is the container of our business limiting us, or can we be expansive like a shoreline within a natural balance? Can we expand our limits without creating pain?

Stretching into Your Comfort Zone

Stretching Into Your Comfort Zone has to do with what you perceive to be possible in a given situation based upon realistic expectations. The comfort zone has a perimeter, and often in yoga, we are twisted to our own personal limit, otherwise known as "the edge." When we play *at* our edge, play *with* our edge, *soften* our edge, and *expand* our edge, we can invite in the breath and create space to take ourselves beyond our limits, and past our edge. We can change it from a hard, sharp, limiting edge to a soft, fluid, expandable edge. Is this not what the best leaders do? Stretching Into Your Comfort Zone means staying with foundational, safe, comfortable areas (areas that you know that you know; conscious competence) and trusting what you know as a leader. It is knowing your capacity, within your limitations. It is also recognizing the capacity for change, both within yourself, your team, and your organization. Stretching within your comfort zone grants you access to choosing when it might be beneficial or strategic to stretch beyond your comfort zone.

What do you notice is inside and outside of your comfort zone as a leader? Discovering your boundaries is a part of the yoga journey as well as the leadership journey. Being humble and confident at the same time is one outcome of learning your comfort zone. Once you really know where you're comfortable, if you slow the action down you'll start to discover where you're vulnerable, where there is weakness in the foundation. You'll begin knowing yourself – knowing how you get to know yourself, and getting that solidified. Yoga is an access point to that, and it's a critical muscle of leadership.

Stretched, Comfortable and Being In the Zone

NOW you can imagine having the proper perspective to prepare to lead in the desired direction of your intention.

Warrior One is emblematic of someone in a leadership position who is totally comfortable in her own skin, in her own head and in the company of others, whether the others offer a community of total support or the fruitful realm of conflict.

Finding one's self "in the zone" fits a definition of flow, loosely defined as that moment when the desired action is congruent with the preceding preparation.

In yoga, as in leadership, the ability to achieve success in any given situation has everything to do with our relationship to being in the moment and finding the flow: "that ideal state of mind associated with achievement or optimal performance... overachieving while feeling terrific, no pain, in the zone, on autopilot, very focused. The fundamentals of flow are absence of fear, awareness of objectives, clarity of goals, effortless motion, unambiguous feedback, concentration on the task, central control, loss of self-consciousness, and time warp (everything slows down)." (from Jackson & Csikszentmihalyi, 1999 Biofeedback, edited by Schwartz and Andrasik, p. 564-65)

Compare the optimal conditions for leadership and the internal art of yoga: confidence (absence of fear), perspective (awareness of objectives), vision (clarity of goals), and focus (concentration on the task).

Perhaps the most under-rated, under-valued and unrecognized characteristic of being in the zone is that of a time warp, where everything seems to slow down. In yoga, this quality of timelessness is highly desired and sought after. In leadership circles, where speed is valued, it can distinguish visionary leaders from run-of-the-mill leaders. The best leaders have mastered this timelessness as an ability to slow down in order to speed up. In reality, it is in this space that yoga asks us to reside...and we ask you to consider it as a saving grace for chaotic times.

"In a society that demands life at double time, speed and addictions numb us to our own experience. In such a society it is almost impossible to settle into our bodies or stay connected with our hearts, let alone connect with one another or the earth where we live."

~Jack Kornfield

And so we move to the next posture...

ASANA #6: *Virabhadrasana II*, Heroic Warrior Pose II

Envision: The warrior, the leader, the athlete, or the politician with the tools of the craft in hand, the embodiment of readiness. Well prepared, fully focused, armed with skills and a strong sense of purpose and conviction, mesmerizing. Total concentration, immersed with purpose, ready to act; embracing that which is desired, with full absorption.

Core Leadership:

- Total Capacity for Leadership at the Right Moment

Leadership Point of View:

- Skills, Mastery

- Perspective, Institutional History

- Grounded and ready for action

- Unflappable

Yogic Point of View:

- *Citta*, the well-developed mind, the mental requirement • *Bhakti*, devotion

- *Tapas*, dedication and devotion

- *Pratyahara*: a quality of withdrawing the senses from the outer world and fully experiencing the inner territory of the mind, allowing an inner awareness to emerge

- *Aparigraha*: non-clinging to outcome, preparing for the best, allowing what will be to be without pre-judging

How to practice Warrior II:

Return to Warrior I: This is the archer, the warrior holding the bow. Now, you become the arrow, steadfast and focused on the future. Bring your right arm forward and left arm back, both extended straight and parallel to the ground, gaze gently ahead. Breathe into your belly, draw the low belly back toward

JASPER JOHAL

your spine, and continue to bend the front knee into a right angle. Root the left foot firmly into the foundation of this pose and from that point, feel the energy of your leg draw up into the core of your being.

The longer you hold this posture, the longer you will experience the precious nature of finding your capacity in the comfort zone of Warrior II. No pain means no pain. If you feel pain, back off. Never over-effort. Breathe.

The arrow faces the uncertainty of the future head-on. The archer holds the choice of being too focused on the future, thus becoming unsteady or uncomfortable or burned- out, with too much emphasis on what "might happen," and less connection with what's happening NOW. Stay grounded, both legs rooted, heart rising. You have to pull in from the past, pull in from the future to fully empower the ability to lead in the moment.

The difficulty of being in the pose comes not from the spatial and temporal relationship of forward and backward, but from the inevitable pull off center, from side to side. Leaders look at the future, informed by the past, but the attacks from all sides by board members, media crises, market influences and public opinion can throw any leader off balance.

The leader's weight has to be equally balanced between the past and the future.

ASANA #7: *Virabhadrasana III*, Warrior III

We know leadership is about action and results. You wouldn't be a leader if you didn't already know how to produce both. You are masterful at setting things in motion, at getting the job done. Let's look at it in terms of the yoga of leadership.

Envision ACTION: The arrow flies, the words are spoken, the order is given, the command is shouted, the count-down reaches "three-two-one...", the IPO is offered, the merger is legal, the deal is sealed.

Core Leadership:

• Capacity for Leadership at the Right Moment

• Ability of the flow of energy to follow its path, to evolve and transform, to create change

Leadership Point of View:

- Skills, Mastery, Prescience
- Perspective, Institutional History
- Action

Yogic Point of View:

- *Citta*, the well-developed mind, the mental requirement
- *Bhakti*, devotion
- *Tapas*, dedication and determination
- *Aparigraha*: non-clinging to outcome, preparing for the best, allowing what will be to be without pre-judging
- *Ishwara pranidhana* ~ reaching beyond one's self for a greater good

How to practice Warrior III:

From Warrior II, swing the back arm forward and reach into the future, allowing the back leg to stretch long behind you while both arms reach out, as if towards a target.

This is a supreme balancing pose, as well as an exercise in stability, steadfastness and courage. It is the ultimate act of bravery: to move from the creation of a set of skills, fine-tuning your tools, and ACTING.

The archer, the bow and arrows, the target.

The leader, the ideas and the skills, the vision. Have you remembered to breathe?

MICHAEL WINOKUR

Reflections:

Stretch Objectives: Moving from the Known to the Unknown

The analogy here for leaders is clear. Leaders must constantly challenge themselves and their people to see beyond the expected, to see new futures and possibilities; to reach, stretching into the unknown, often uncomfortable territory. It takes a willingness to play at that edge since too may leaders have learned the lesson of asking their people for too much for too long, resulting in pain, exhaustion, burnout and failure.

The challenge for leaders is not to be competitive, not to be pushing. There is a distinction between playing the edge and competition. Leaders often get competitive instead of playing their own edge. Ironically, it is this ability to *play the edge* versus *compete to win* that actually provides a competitive edge and unfair advantage in the marketplace. Steve Jobs was able to transform Apple's business model by expanding the edge of the comfort zone of the former computer company and revolutionizing the music and entertainment market and ultimately the mobile phone market. This gave Apple the competitive edge to innovate and therefore skyrocket their success, leaving competitors to scramble to catch up. Apple didn't win by competing to win. Apple won by stretching and expanding the comfort zone; playing the edge.

Finding Center on the Edge

One of the key principles is that playing your edge is about being very centered as a human being; it isn't about struggle. Yoga and leadership are both very much about an internal conversation. It's not about struggle, it's not about effort, it's about the awareness of the space between your comfort zone and stretching into that edge, without going over into pain or accepting discomfort. It's subtle, but the distinction is about stretching into comfort rather than enduring pain. Developing awareness that the edge is not pain, it is finding the place of intensity, of exquisite intensity - but not pain. Yoga is not about pain, it is finding and working at your edge. It is a relaxed state of intensity, which to many leaders will sound like an oxymoron, but yoga teaches us that it is a choice we can consciously make. How long do we allow ourselves (both in yoga and in business) to stay uncomfortable? Real leadership is challenging, a place of exquisite intensity and complexity, but needn't be about pain. Today we see far too many leaders in pain, folks who have forgotten how to breathe lightness and joy into the act of leading.

Seeing the Value in Action without Clinging to Expectations

In yoga, we discover that being clear on your intention while at the same time letting go is often how we can access an otherwise difficult pose. This is counter-intuitive to everything people in business are trained to do. Try on this leadership application: the concept of playing the edge, of non-effort, of clarity to intention without attachment, of letting go. Most people think letting go means defeat, but it means crafting and sustaining an openness that the possibility may show up in a different way. Leaders get stuck in the limiting belief that there's a right path to the goal, one way to do things. Think of an example where you might feel stuck in your own work. See if you can let go of the approach you've been assuming was the right or only way to do it and allow an alternate option to emerge. Question assumptions.

Yoga is ultimately about relationships: your relationship with yourself, your relationship with your inner voices (whether critical, judgmental, congratulatory or kind), your relationship with energy, endurance and resilience. As leaders, it is all about those same relationships as well as self-mastery, relationship with the board, with the media, with stakeholders of all sorts, and relationship with your employees. Leadership is about the integrity of your relationship with other people and yoga prepares you because it is about your relationship with your innermost self. If there is a fluidity and flow between people that you can achieve through managing conscious conversations and energy awareness. Leadership is about influencing in the space of relationships. Results and actions occur in the context of relationships, and the leader's job is to cultivate a sophisticated enough relationship with Self to be able to create the space for others to generate results through relationships.

This very current, flow, and integration is what's missing to help leaders get themselves and their organizations or teams to the next level.

A practice to go to the next level:

Practice the flowing combination of Warrior I, II and III...then settle into the restorative posture of Bridge Pose (described in the next chapter)...bridging the realm of Doing, with the realm of Being.

Chapter Five
Leadership: Perspective and Self-Preservation

The ancient concepts of yin and yang relate to both yoga, as you'd expect, and leadership. Yang is the more active, engaged, doing side and yin is more restful, restorative, still, and peaceful. Both in balance create flow for leaders and yoga practitioners. Up to this point, our thoughts and practices have been driven by an intensity to know, to understand the territory, to create balance and stability, to fine tune skill sets and sharpen our capacity to use specific tools within the outer world of leadership circles and the inner world of self-awareness on the yoga mat. Ours has been an active pursuit, physically demanding and intellectually engaging. This is the *yang* of yin-yang, the active, dominant force of nature.

Now, we turn to the yin-side, the quiet, nurturing, reflective practice.

Setu is a bridge, in Sanskrit. It is that which connects two places that are somehow separate, as banks of a river or distant shore points. Bridges also traverse space, such as a viaduct. Bridges are usually elevated and overcome some obstacle to the normal flow of things, commerce, movement, materials, even ideas. Cultural bridges aspire to overcome differences, dental bridges add bite where it's been lost and bridges between bank accounts help you avoid overdraft charges. The breath is the bridge between body and mind.

This next yoga posture is intended to bridge the space between an active, yang practice, as epitomized by the *Virabhadrasana* series of postures (Warrior series), and the yin practices of

Nataraj and *Savasana*, the final resting pose of every yoga session.

Asana #8: *Setu Banda*, Bridge Pose

> Envision: A beautiful bridge adjoining two very different landscapes.

Your body, stretched out on the floor, head and shoulders relax on the ground while the hips and belly lift skyward, knees bent, feet firmly planted.

CEOs shaking hands over the completion of a merger. Major projects coming to an end. A surgeon closing up after a successful surgery. Dusk and dawn. The moment between fury and forgiveness, confusion and understanding, wanting and having.

Core Leadership Concept:

- Maintaining a strong connection throughout the process, all parties united

- Creating stability, maintaining commitments, supreme reliability

Leadership Point of View:

- Congruence and how you make meaningful transitions

- Relationship between leader and stakeholders

Yogic Point of View:

- Integral connections between knowing and not knowing, having and not-having

- • Time to regroup, reconnect the body with the mind through the bridge of the breath

- Relationship of past, present and future ~ Transcendence

How to practice Bridge Pose:

Begin by stretching out on your back with legs bent so that your feet rest flat on the floor; this will protect your lumbar spine and relieve tension and tightness in the hips and sacrum. Feel your head and neck relax as your shoulders rest firmly on the floor. Feel the chest rise and fall with the breath. Place your arms alongside the body, bend your elbows so that your forearms extend upwards, perpendicular to the floor, and open the hands so the palms feel stretched and fingers radiate out like rays of sunlight. Strongly press your triceps toward the floor keeping the neck soft and tongue relaxed.

Press your feet downward; root your shoulders and lift your hips and ribs away from the floor in one smooth and gentle movement. Breathe deeply. Hold the pose, or support your sacrum on a yoga block, small ball, or wrapped up towel. No pain is no pain. Repeat three times. Feel the flow of energy from your belly to your brain, and from your hips to your toes. Be the bridge between breaths. Be the bridge between thoughts. Be the bridge for the self-emergent phenomenon to evolve....Just Be.

YOGA is the recognition that energy flows, always has and always will, that is all. Nothing else really matters. Yoga tells us that beyond the known and knowable, there is the unknown and unknowable.

Seeking the source of the flow, that deep wellspring of inspiration, the yoga teacher offers the invitation: "soften your awareness so you can feel the flow of energy within. Place your hand over your heart...feel the flow, here..."

MICHAEL WINOKUR

She suggests ways that you might do that:

• soften your awareness, soften your skin

• embrace stillness, Be stillness

• flow with your breath, pause at the top and bottom of every breath, dwell there

Again, totally counter-intuitive to modern leaders who had to drive, leaning forward, never stopping, always moving to get to the top.

More of what's missing to get leaders to next level: More stillness, more time for introspection, more time to bridge the gaps...

You need time to slow the action down enough to become aware of the tension in your shoulders and the annoyance in your voice, to slow the action down enough to feel the reaction in your gut before reacting ....to ask "what am I feeling?"....to notice, to breathe, to pause before reacting and before reactioning.....to choose the response mindfully.

Congruence and Alignment

Great Leaders, like great actors, know how to use their emotion to express their ideas and passions in ways that are congruent and create impact, skills that can only be accomplished with the kind of self observation and awareness that yogis learn to use in expressing congruity in their poses: both take quieting the mind of self judgment and other noise to focus on a simple observation of the moment....being in and one with the moment.

Power of Inversion

Bridge pose is an inversion, and one of the childlike joys of yoga is inversions. As kids, we flip our bodies around for fun, we hang upside down off the edge of beds and at the playground, we lay on the floor and look at cracks in the ceiling, imagining the ceiling is the floor and we have to walk carefully around the light fixture and step over the doorjamb to go into the next room. We lay on the grass and look at the clouds, imagining shapes. Where do we get to do these things as grown-ups at work? This is one of the joys of yoga, where we regularly shift our perspective and view the world from various uncommon positions. We stand on our heads and hands, we twist ourselves around and under our own arms, we bend at the waist and twist to look around our own ankles to the view behind us. The world, and life, looks different from these different angles.

Shifting Leadership Point of View

As creatures of habit, we have our favorite seat in the conference room, "our" seat at the dinner table. Our worldview or leadership point of view (LPOV) has a lot to do with our position. Where you sit in an organization determines how things look to you. The CEO has a very different view than the receptionist or line worker. The HR exec has a different leadership point of view than does the sales leader. The head of procurement and the comptroller will also have different perspectives on the organization. By putting yourself in a different position, whether it is in the boardroom or yoga studio, you can expand your thinking and see new options and solutions. Change your position and see what opens up! In your next controversy or thorny problem to solve as a team, or when you feel stuck, simply get up and take a different chair or stand in a different part of the room. See if things look different from there. Or, put yourself metaphorically in the minds' eye of the person you feel most opposed to. Who is the most against your point of view? Can you put yourself in his or her position to get a different perspective yourself? Can you see how they got to their current way of thinking? Seek to understand how they got to their current position. From this new position/view, can you see how to move the conversation forward? Can you create a viable argument for the other's cause? Can you argue for the opposing position?

Chapter Six
The Dance of Creation and Control, that which a Leader Does Best

*Often leaders must choose to destroy before being able to build. What we create and sustain we **must also destroy and build anew**.*

Knowing + expressing who you are + revealing capabilities = attracts others

If the goal is total expression of one's self, then we must talk about change, about creativity and its consequential destructiveness.

It's the dance of control.

We want control.

We seek it, we find it, we use it, we lose it.

The cycle of renewal and destruction allows for creation. You create, then you sustain or maintain what you've created, whether it's a yoga pose or a company. Your belief in your self and your work, the strength of your conviction, your knowledge and experience are the Breath of Life from which positive change can flow…it is foundational to everything.

You set the pose, you blossom into the pose, you use your breath, and embrace the reality that it is impermanent, everything is impermanent. Inhale doesn't happen without exhale. Up doesn't happen without down. Thus, create doesn't happen without destroy. If you've had any longevity in your organization or current work, you know that businesses, like people, both inhale and exhale. You have to exhale just as all things must end. You as a leader can decide when you want to end or change, in fact that's core to strategy...knowing when it is time to destroy and build anew. It is a natural cycle of breath, of business, of yoga.

When you come from that place of knowing, what does it really mean to gamble? You know what the risks are. You assess your risks and any investor knows you have to have, at some level, a willingness to lose. That cycle of the control dance is as natural as breathing. What we create and sustain we must also destroy and build anew. That becomes the practice of evolution and is no longer caught up in cycles of success and failure, good and bad. The light and dark of yoga, just like the light and dark of business, is that cycle of renewal and destruction. If we as individuals and as businesses have peace as our objective, that would have us avoid conflict. If we avoid conflict, we will not survive, and survival is what we are all here to do. Peace is an agreement, an understanding, approval, and acknowledgement of common values. Rather, what we really want is harmony. Harmony allows for the dark side. It is about alignment and the understanding that sometimes, in order to survive, something must be destroyed.

In yoga we celebrate lightness while at the same time we honor and recognize darkness. As a leader you must confront and know your own dark side, your own destructive tendencies, your own shadow self. As a leader, too, you must have keen awareness of the dark side of your organization, your people, your board, the market, etc. The global business ethic that's emerging in our century is all about the company, not people, not community, not social consciousness. But you, as a leader, understand that you must honor the individual, create and nurture a vital sense of belonging in a healthy community with a strong social conscience.

Asana #9: *Nataraja*, The Divine Dancer.

Natarajasana, Dancer of Creation and Destruction

Envision this: You stand within the fiery framework of your life, built with a passion for leadership... You stand tall.

Core Leadership Concept:

- Capacity to destroy, create, sustain, dissolve and recreate

Leadership Point of View:

- Perspective, Institutional History

Yogic Point of View:

- Everything changes, nothing remains the same
- We have the power to change that which must be changed
- Destruction is good, necessary, natural

How to practice Divine Dancer Pose:

Breathe in, hands in *anjali mudra* in front of your heart. Exhale, arms release outward. Energy flows from the center of your awareness as if it would ignite the fingertips, so that as you breathe in again and sweep your arms up and overhead, it is as if you are igniting a fiery frame for your pose, for your work, for your relationships, for your life.

Lift your left leg, bend the knee and- move it into a diagonal direction, like a Balinese dancer, outward to the left, in the act of creating anew. Extend your left hand forward, as if to shake someone's hand, in reassurance, the right hand defiant in front of the heart in *abhaya*, the *mudra* of fearlessness.

CHRIS ANDRE

At first, your arms are reaching away, pull them in toward your center to reestablish a strong sense of center, from which your energy can emanate outward, and pulse inward again, feeling the throb and vibration of your zest for life.

Be willing to fall, and fail, to rebuild again and again and again; be consciously aware of the possibilities of falling and recovering as a cycle and process for finite learning. A state of ultimate allowing. Lighten up around mistakes and failure. Be willing to put something on the table for the third, fourth, or fifth time, stay in difficult conversations, or stay in the inquiry without resolution.

Remain focused on breathing and maintaining balance, stay in your body. Breathe deeply and steadily; recognize the nature of positive change and your commitment to it, allow it to transform your attachment to the present moment ~ be here, tall and graceful, potent and empowered.

Effortless Engagement

Aligning with your authentic self in your leadership style is how you will bring balance to your boldness, by allowing lightness and ease to illuminate your role as a leader. It requires giving up effort and struggle and relying on those practices that keep you grounded, aligned with your commitments, building on your strengths, and letting go of attachment, outcomes, unnecessary or blinding seriousness so that you can find the place of lightness, breath, effortlessness and joy in your leadership mastery.

Chapter Seven
Internal Politics — Residing Within

Envision, imagine:

A Woman, or a Man, in business attire, and very tired. Ahhh, yes, it is YOU.

You are stretched out on the floor with your legs up the wall. You are breathing quietly, long deep and gentle breaths...with long pauses at the top and bottom of every breath. And in that space between each breath, there are no thoughts.

Imagine that.

In the adrenaline-junkie, 24-7 wi-fi pace of our business lives today, when does the leader allow the shifting sands to settle long enough to see what's transpired? There's a point at the end of every yoga practice where you lay still on the ground, on your back, eyes closed, and allow the energy of all that you've just done integrate within your body. It's a restful time. A peaceful time.

The final yoga of leadership pose is this:

Asana #10: *Savasana*, (pronounced "shi-vasana") Corpse Pose

Core Leadership Concept:

- Sustainability through simplicity

Leadership Point of View:

- Positioning for scalability depends on recovery and renewal

- You can't do it all without the balance that *savasana* brings –

- Can YOU find *savasana* in every action?

- The Leader's responsibility is to breathe life into the organization.

Yogic Point of View:

- Energetic reintegration, renewal and awareness of the expansive quality of stillness

- Can you find *savasana* in every pose?

- You are The Breath

Sava, in Sanskrit, is the word for corpse, that which is lifeless, without movement, totally passive. It is the pose that can be invited into every other *asana* as a means of balancing effort with ease, of balancing outer awareness with inner stillness.

You need this.

How to practice this yoga posture:

Stretch out on the floor if you wish, or in a comfortable chair or bed; a floor would be ideal. Use blankets or pillows to create comfort for yourself. Never keep yourself in an uncomfortable position in yoga, or in work or life for that matter with a colleague, coworker or spouse. All of us can endure an enormous amount of discomfort ~ you wouldn't have gotten THIS far in life without being able to endure a great deal of discomfort! You do not need to prove this point in your yoga practice or leadership role.

Once you are comfortable, soften the breath, feel the rise and fall of your rib cage, the gentle expansion and contraction of your chest and belly.

Relax the space between your eyebrows, between your eyebrows and hairline. Relax the space beside your eyes, between your nose and lips; relax your tongue and jaw; relax the base of your skull, neck and throat. Soften the spaces between your shoulders, elbows, wrists and fingertips. Relax the front body and back body, along the side-body and belly, between your hips. Relax your thighs and knees; the spaces behind your knees, your ankles and the spaces between your toes.

Sense the flow of energies, flesh and blood, breath and thoughts, and return your awareness to the breath, only the breath. Notice that your breath is cool as you breathe in, warm as you breathe out and allow the breath to breathe you. Just that. For five minutes or more.

Be the Observer

Start with that, simply observe yourself in *Savasana*. Simply observe yourself in relationship with your self. Without criticizing how you are doing, without analyzing or judging, without evaluating or trying to quantify it.

RICHARD CUMMINGS

You are, after all is said and done, just a vessel, filled with light. A beacon, a lighthouse, a refuge.

Most people are constitutionally incapable of slowing down to self-observe. The normal orientation is to an active drive for results. Or the orientation is to get people to produce results. Or the orientation is to fix the problem. Rarely do we observe the relationship between what's even previous to our behavior, what produces our behavior. It is so important to learn to see what you can't see, which is to see yourself in action and how your attitude or your emotional space or your judgment or your evaluation actually impacts your next action. But you rarely see that process, because that's not where your attention is. There's always someone trying to get you to do something, trying to motivate you, trying to get you to go somewhere.

Learn to observe your self without harsh judgment or even positive judgment; to do that, you have to see the judgment. Yoga and meditation are keys to gaining the ability to witness, to simply observe the workings of your mind. This quality of the self to observe without judgment is a fundamental key to yoga, and to healthy and productive relationships in the world of business.

Herbert Benson, of Harvard Medical School and founder of the Benson-Henry Institute for Mind Body medicine at Massachusetts General Hospital makes this so simple in his writings and research captured in his book, *Relaxation Revolution*. Here's his recommendation, his prescription for finding *savasana* in one minute:

> The Mini-Relaxation Response Technique
>
> * Take a deep breath and hold it for about 7-10 seconds
>
> * Exhale completely, and as you do so, silently repeat your focus word or phrase* * This entire procedure should take no more than 10-15 seconds.
>
> * Continue to breathe regularly, and proceed with your normal activities.

That single *focus word or phrase* carries your intention for calmness, peace, joy, relief and can be any of those particular words or any other word or phrases that make you feel good. They can be totally your own creation or idea, lines or mantras that convey your heart's desire, your quest for deep inner awareness and serenity.

Begin Again: The Ultimate Secrets are Always the Most Obvious, Simple and Magical

So much of yoga is about pointing your toes in the direction you want your body to go and then learning to relax and arrive there rather than straining to get it right. It's amazing when you do get there, but the point is to relax enough to enjoy where you are in the moment, wherever your body is that day. Leadership is like that. All you can do is point all the resources in the direction you want the organization to go, align everyone with the vision of where you're headed, and then relax and enjoy where you are at each moment, trusting that it will get there eventually: enjoying wherever you are. Being in the moment. Mastering the beginner's mind. Approach it all as a beginner and enjoy, revel in the process. Have the very process be nurturing. Turn the normal thing on its end.

There's no place to go.

You've already arrived.

About The Authors

SUZI POMERANTZ

Suzi Pomerantz, MT, MCC is an award-winning master leadership coach, facilitator, and author with 25 years of executive coaching experience working with leaders and teams in over 200 organizations internationally: government agencies, not-for-profit and private sector clients, including seven companies on the Fortune 100 list. She is the CEO of Innovative Leadership International LLC, the founder of the Leading Coaches' Center, and co-Founder of the Library of Professional Coaching.

A strategic thought partner to executives and entrepreneurs, Suzi's strength lies in helping leaders and organizations find clarity within chaos. She was one of the first to be awarded the Master Certified Coach credential, which is the highest international commendation awarded to coaches by the

International Coaching Federation, and has maintained it for over 20 years. She is considered a thought leader in the coaching industry and is known as "a game changer."

A recognized leader passionate about excellence, integrity, legacy, impact, and leadership excellence in organizations and stewardship of the profession of coaching, Suzi serves in a number of international Board of Director positions and volunteer leadership roles, donating time and resources to organizations that are leading the future of the coaching profession. She was the founding Vice President of the International Consortium for Coaching in Organizations (ICCO) and served on the Advisory Board after two terms on the Executive Board. She was also a founding board member of the International Journal for Coaching in Organizations (IJCO). Suzi has been guest faculty and a featured speaker to industry leaders in more than a dozen coaching schools and communities worldwide.

Suzi presented as well as participated for seven years as an Executive Board Member and past co-Chairman of the International Executive Coaching Summit, an invitation-only annual gathering of worldwide senior executive development experts. She presented at the Annual International Coach Federation Conference, and the World Business and Executive Coach Summit, and taught executive coaches as faculty at the Executive Coach Academy and the College of Executive Coaching. She has also delivered guest lectures at George Washington University, Loyola University, and the University of Virginia and has coached executives in the MBA for Executives Program at the University of Virginia Darden School of Business. Suzi presented, coached, and led team meetings at the prestigious Linkage Best of Organizational Development Summit.

Suzi is credited with over30publications about coaching, ethics, and business development, and 9 books including the bestseller *Seal the Deal*. She was named a SupporTED coaching hero for her work with world-changing leaders in the prestigious TED Fellowship program. In 2012 she was invited to the Advisory Council of Harvard Business Review. She's been practicing yoga for over 12 years and is the mother of two teens. She lives in the Washington, DC metro area with her husband of 20 years. Learn more at http://InnovativeLeader.com .

LINDA LANG

Linda Lang's studio, The Open Door, has brought yoga into the greater Washington community since 1999. During that time her work has been recognized and recommended by Shady Grove Adventist Hospital's Wellness Program and the Center for Integrative Medicine at the George Washington University Medical Center in Washington, D.C.

She is a frequent lecturer at GWU's Medical School on subjects of therapeutic applications of yoga and meditation, student and community wellness.

Linda is certified in the medical arena of Cardiac Yoga, is an Anusara-Inspired instructor and serves as a guest lecturer on stress management, yoga and meditation. She presents classes, workshops and seminars throughout the year for the George Washington University Medical School, and is adjunct faculty in the undergraduate Lifestyle, Sport and Physical Activity Program. Linda has taught at The Center for Holistic Psychiatry, the Discovery Channel, non-profit organizations and numerous educational institutions.

She holds the professional designation with the national Yoga Alliance as E-RYT ~ for "teachers with significant teaching experience who want to train teachers or conduct continuing education." Given this expertise, Linda joined the International Association of Yoga Therapists.

In addition to teaching, Linda is engaged in research projects demonstrating the benefits of yoga as a life style choice, as personal and professional skill development and as a palliative modality.

She belongs to Peaceable Dragon, a consortium of teachers and students exploring Yoga, Qi Gong, Taijiquan (Tai Chi), Aikido, meditation and other internal arts.

Linda has studied yoga extensively with John Friend, as well as Doug Keller, Martin Kirk, Betsey Downing, Desiree Rambaugh and Todd Norian. Sally Kempton and Richard Miller have been influential in the study of meditation and yoga nidra.

Linda works with the **Center for Integrative Medicine at George Washington University Hospital** as a member of their team of health care practitioners and medical professionals.

Linda is a dedicated teacher with a comprehensive perspective, offering public and private classes.

Linda's fascination with yoga began 45 years ago, when the Beatles brought Maharishi Mahesh Yogi into the spotlight. Since that time, 1967 to be precise, she has been drawn to eastern literature, art and philosophy, the fundamentals and foundations of classical yoga traditions. Today, she is a highly trained professional, certified in the medical arena of Cardiac Yoga, with an appointment as adjunct faculty in the Department of Psychiatry and Behavioral Medicine at GWU-SMHSR.

In 2009, Linda was invited to join the Center for Integrative Medicine at the George Washington University School of Medicine and Health Sciences Research in Washington, D.C., as their Therapeutic Yoga practitioner. In addition to being a frequent lecturer and instructor at GWU's Medical School on therapeutic applications of yoga and meditation, she is a popular presenter at seminars and retreats on medical leadership and professional development, as well as student and community wellness.

Linda is known for her innovative and creative contributions to the field of therapeutic yoga and yoga therapy, as founder and director of Therapeutic Yoga of Greater Washington. Her original, ground-breaking curriculum designs are a result of collaboration with medical schools in search of meaningful ways to bring non-traditional, integrative modalities into personal, academic, community and clinical settings.

She serves as community and committee member with the Consortium of Academic Health Centers for Integrative Medicine and the Academic Consortium for Complementary and Alternative Health Care, as well as the International Association of Yoga Therapy.

At the moment, Linda serves as consultant to Tai Sophia Institute in Maryland, a leader in wellness education and holistic Eastern medicine, as they prepare to offer a Master's degree program in Therapeutic Yoga. She is also involved with the newly endowed Contemplative Sciences Center at the University of Virginia.

Author's Note:

By the time we met, Linda had been teaching yoga for years ~ a teaching career that blossomed after her children were grown, after years of management consulting, local politics and community advocacy. Together on the mat, Suzi and Linda have experienced the profound impact of yoga in their personal and professional lives. They are together, here, to share the mindfulness and power, the awe and mystery, with you.

No book is ever just born. There's a story behind it; A story of why the book was written and how it came to be. This book had a long journey and emerged in it's own unfolding over time.

In 2004 Suzi stumbled upon yoga after meeting Kathy Thompson (founder of Follow Your Heart Yoga Center) at a Washington Metro Area ICF Coaches meeting in 2004. Kathy had previously been an executive coach, and had left coaching to open her yoga studio in 2004. Here's how it unfolded from there:

"I went to an introductory yoga class that Kathy was teaching, and was surprised to find that the core concepts behind Anusara yoga that were posted on the wall of the yoga studio resonated with my orientation as a leadership coach: Attitude, Alignment, Action. I loved the gentle stretching and focus on breathing, and found that taking a yoga class once a week did wonders for my stress levels as well as my flexibility, strength, and balance. As an entrepreneur and mom of two young kids,

I found yoga to be my oasis of calm in an otherwise uber-busy life. So, I kept going.

The unexpected miracle of yoga was that chronic pain I'd been feeling from a herniated disk in my neck that resulted after a car accident in 1991 actually disappeared as a direct result of the yoga, which creates space between the vertebrae with regular stretching. I was pain-free for the first time in almost 15 years. So, I kept going. After several seasons of yoga with various teachers, I found Linda Lang's class and had an experience that can only be described as transcendent bliss. Something about her yoga instruction got me doing things with my body I'd not done since I was ten (headstands, backbends, and handstands, oh my!), and she miraculously got me out of my head (hence, the transcendent bliss comment). I'm one of those leaders with a very chatty monkey brain who never had much success with meditation before, so this experience of simultaneously calming and elevating my consciousness was unprecedented for me. So, I kept going.

In every class I heard Linda give instructions for various poses, and some part of my brain would whisper, "hey, that's good advice for leaders!", or "wow, that would have a powerful impact on an organization!" At first, I just figured it was coincidence. Then, as it kept happening, I started to pay attention to the wisdom and leadership notes that were disguised as yoga instructions.

It was too consistent to be a coincidence, and for awhile I just amused myself with noticing it and then wondered if it was just me. Was I hearing it that way because of my work as a leadership coach? Do all leadership coaches hear yoga instructions as applicable to leadership, or is that just me? I consulted with my mentor coach and dear friend, Jackie Eiting, over lunch one day in late 2005. Jackie is a brilliant leadership coach and consultant who I knew had been practicing yoga for a few years longer than I had, and what I intended to be a question over lunch came out of my mouth as a declaration instead. I told her I was going to write a book called the Yoga of Leadership about how yoga instructions strike me as profound leadership insights. The intensity and enthusiasm of her response surprised me, and confirmed that it wasn't just me after all. We had such a deep and powerful conversation about it, we immediately decided it would be fun to do together, and that she and I would co-author it. We started it in February of 2006 and then worked on it for two more years, in 2007 and 2008 together, at which point Jackie wanted to shift her focus to other work projects and world travel. We felt we'd taken the manuscript as far as we could, but that we needed the input from a yoga instructor or someone with more yoga mastery than we embodied from our leadership point of view. I offered to approach my friend and yoga instructor, Linda.

Meanwhile, Linda and I had created a deepening friendship with long walks and talks after yoga class and years of practicing yoga together. At first I was shy about sharing the idea with Linda, who has both deep and broad expertise and knowledge in yoga as a practice and an art, as well as the philosophical underpinnings and spiritual and linguistic aspects of the ancient ways of yoga. She's a true yoga master, and on one of our walks I sheepishly shared that I'd been all along hearing her instructions not only as tutelage for the poses, but as wise advice for leaders and powerful coaching for leaders.

That was a turning point in our relationship on many levels. She had a similarly intense and enthusiastic response to Jackie's...an elated, fist-pumping "YES!" that clearly reinforced once again that it wasn't just me thinking this stuff. It turns out Linda has done workshops for CEOs that she appropriately named "CEyOga". She offered to read our manuscript and comment on it from her yogic point of view. Very shortly thereafter, she came on board as co-author and we built more layers of the book together.

By 2009, we started seeing blog posts by other leadership consultants who were making the same links between yoga and leadership, so we knew we were on to something that was wanting to emerge in the business world. By then, Linda and I had completely re-wired the manuscript. Contrary to my natural bias for action and wanting to be first to market with this concept, we agreed that this book, like a yoga practice, would be an emergent phenomenon...meaning it would unfold in it's own time, on it's own journey. Who knew that journey would take ten+ more years? With Linda as my co-author, the meaty yogic context for the leadership insights took shape, and I am forever grateful for her brilliance and gentle spirit.

The result is the book you hold in your hands today. We fervently hope that you, whether you are a leader, a yoga practitioner, a coach, or someone who's never taken a yoga class in your life, have found enormous insight, wisdom, value, and calm in these pages.

Namaste.

When times are tough, tough leaders apply the Yoga of Leadership.

Access the secret that makes a great leader into an Exceptional Leader.

The key is The Yoga of Leadership.

- As a leader, do you feel overwhelmed, overcrowded, and overworked?
- Wonder why time seems to be speeding up?
- Is the speed and pace of the workplace today making you nuts?
- Do you ever wonder why you can't relax, even on vacation?
- Is this 24-7 plugged-in, turned-on life really all it's cracked up to be?
- Didn't work used to be more fun, more challenging, more satisfying? What happened?
- Why can't you slow down?
- You are successful….how come you still worry?
- You are successful ….why can't you enjoy it more?
- When you talk and move faster, are you more efficient? More productive?
- What does yoga have to do with leadership?

In this quick, yet evocative airplane read, we reveal the secrets that combat the distractions of the current speed-addicted, efficiency-crazed culture bred from technology, global competition, and market conditions. All those driven, excitement-junkie, edgy, efficient-to-a-fault, multi-tasking, run-run-run executives we know and love have something in common that prevents them from being the exceptional leaders we know they can be… THEY DON'T BREATHE!

This book enables leaders to achieve mastery through personal transformation of the internal landscape (i.e., mindset shifts), increased awareness, and making explicit the parallels between yoga principles and exceptional leadership…a primer for the very successful, on the way up, or 'arrived' business Executive.

www.ingramcontent.com/pod-product-compliance
Lightning Source LLC
Chambersburg PA
CBHW021441210526
45463CB00002B/602